Originally published in Amsterdam by the Averroès Foundation, under the title *Sjamsi en Ali Baba in de stad*

Text: © 1994 Ghazi Abdel-Qadir
Illustrations: © 1994 Alice Hoogstad
English version © 1997 by the High/Scope Educational Research Foundation.
All rights reserved. Except as permitted under the Copyright Act of 1976, no part of this book may be reproduced or distributed in any form or by any means, electronic or mechanical, including photocopy, recording, or any information storage-or-retrieval system, without prior written permission from the publisher. High/Scope is a registered trademark and service mark of the High/Scope Educational Research Foundation.

English version translation by Eric van Deventer

English version published by
HIGH/SCOPE PRESS
A division of
High/Scope Educational Research Foundation
600 North River Street
Ypsilanti, Michigan 48198-2898
(313)485-2000, FAX (313)485-0704

Library of Congress CIP#: 97-23379
ISBN: 1-57379-070-2

10 9 8 7 6 5 4 3 2 1

Ghazi Abdel-Qadir

Sjamsi and Ali Baba in Town

Illustrations by Alice Hoogstad

Series Editor: David P. Weikart

a division of High/Scope Educational Research Foundation

Ypsilanti, Michigan

"Sjamsi! Time to go!" called his mother.
Sjamsi was very excited.
He was going to town with his mother for the first time!
He ran into the courtyard to catch
Ali Baba, his rooster. Ali Baba was his best friend.

"Here we are!" said Sjamsi. "We are ready to go."

"We?" asked Mother. "Ali Baba and I, of course," answered Sjamsi.

"Do you want to take along the rooster?" asked his mother.

"Well, of course; he has never been to town either."

"Just like me," observed Sjamsi.

"Putt, putt." The bus came around the corner.
Sjamsi and his mother got on board.
They sat down, and Sjamsi got to sit next to the window.
"You'll have to hold on tight to Ali Baba," said his mother.

Oh, how exciting it was in town!
Sjamsi wanted to stop at every shop and look at everything.
But his mother pulled him along with her.
Ali Baba became quite upset because of all the noise,
and he crowed very loudly, "Cock-a-doodle-doo. Cock-a-doodle-doo."

Sjamsi's mother wanted to buy food at the grocery store.
"No roosters allowed in here!" warned the grocer.
"Why not?" asked Sjamsi. "Ali is very nice."
"Nice roosters don't exist," growled the grocer.

So Sjamsi and Ali Baba had to stay outside.
"Wait here for me," said Sjamsi's mother.
"And don't go anywhere else."
Sjamsi didn't mind waiting.
There was enough to see outside.

"Berry pudding! Red berry pudding!" cried a merchant.

"Crumb cake! Delicious sweet crumb cake!" called another.

"Cotton candy, as thin as girls' hair!" sang a third man, offering his wares. Sjamsi felt his mouth water.

Sjamsi wanted to buy a piece of the crumb cake.

He had a coin somewhere.

He searched all his pockets, but he couldn't find the coin anywhere.

He put Ali Baba down for just a moment so he could look again.

Immediately the rooster fluttered away.

"Ali Baba! Ali Baba!" shouted Sjamsi loudly.
"Come here!"
But Ali Baba didn't listen to him.
The rooster ran down the busy street.
Luckily, Ali Baba wasn't run down
when he darted in front of a car.

11

Sjamsi ran after Ali Baba.
"Stop that rooster! Stop that rooster!" he called out as he ran.
But Ali Baba was much too fast.
He knew how to get away.
Ali Baba was almost caught by a girl,
but at the last moment he made his escape.

Ali Baba disappeared under a peach merchant's booth.
"Get away, you naughty fowl!" scolded the merchant while
he kicked at him. But instead of kicking Ali Baba, he hit his stall support.
The stall fell down and the peaches rolled all over the ground.

"Whose rooster is that anyway?"
shouted the angry peach merchant
as he ran after Ali Baba.
He caught him by his tail feathers and growled,
"Now I have you, you nasty fowl!"
But Ali Baba knew how to escape, and he slipped away.

And on went the chase.
Children screamed and people jumped out of the way.
Ali Baba fluttered close to a lady who was selling strawberries.
Startled, she let her basket fall, and the
red strawberries bounced all over the street.

Now the strawberry saleslady joined the chase!

"Just you wait 'til I get you!" she screamed.

"I am going to make you into soup."

"Oh, no!" thought Sjamsi anxiously. "Run, Ali Baba, run! Make soup of him? Never!"

Rather than that, he would let Ali Baba go free and never see him again.

Ali Baba ran away as fast as he could.
There were three big bowls of whipping cream at a milkman's stand.
Ali Baba landed right in the middle of one of the bowls.
Whipping cream spattered everywhere, as the milkman
pulled the rooster out of the bowl.

"You have spoiled a whole bowl of whipping cream!" he shouted and shook poor Ali Baba to and fro. "That will cost you your head!"

"Oh, no!" screamed Sjamsi. "That is my rooster!"

"I am going to make him into soup!" yelled the strawberry saleslady.

"I can't sell my strawberries because of that rooster."

"No, he's mine!" shouted the peach merchant.

All the merchants started quarreling about who was going to make soup out of Ali Baba. Sjamsi wondered in despair how he could save his rooster. Finally, the merchants decided to go to the lady who was the market judge.

The judge told the merchants, "You can make jam out of the peaches.
You can make syrup out of the strawberries.
But you can't make anything out of the spoiled whipping cream.
Therefore, milkman, the rooster is yours."

"Hooray!" shouted the milkman. "Today I am going to eat roasted rooster!"

Just then Sjamsi got an idea.
"No, don't roast Ali Baba!" he begged.
"I have a better idea. Why don't you sell a fruit salad made from the fruit and top it with the last of the whipping cream?"
"What a brilliant idea!" declared the judge.

"But you won't get the rooster back until I have earned my money," said the milkman, and he put Ali Baba in a dark box.
When the fruit salad was ready, Sjamsi advertised it.
"Fruit salad! Delicious sweet fruit salad!" he called.
And lots of people bought it.

It didn't take long before the enormous bowl was nearly empty and all the merchants were satisfied. Then Sjamsi was allowed to take back Ali Baba.
"But how do I find my mother?" he asked fearfully.
"If you can tell us where she might be, then we will go and find her," said the judge, much to Sjamsi's relief.
"We also want to meet the mother of such a bright boy."

"My mother is in the grocery shop," said Sjamsi.

"But there is one on every street corner," said the peach merchant. "Is that all you know?" "Well, across from the grocery shop three merchants sell a lot of delicious things to eat," recalled Sjamsi.

"Delicious things!" sighed the milkman.
"Delicious things are sold all over the place!"
"Also, there was a lemonade merchant wearing a green turban," added Sjamsi rapidly.
"Oh, that is grandfather Moesa!" exclaimed the strawberry saleslady.
"Now I know where your mother is. I will go and bring her."

Sjamsi's mother enjoyed the last dish of the fruit salad.
She was surprised as she listened to the story of Ali Baba, and the adventure with the fruits and the whipping cream.
Afterward, Sjamsi took a handful of grain from his pocket and offered it to his beloved rooster. Ali Baba ate all the grain from his hand, stretched his neck, and crowed very loudly,

"Cock-a-doodle-doo! Cock-a-doodle-doo! Cock-a-doodle-doo!"